Common Sense

Mentoring

Insights and answers for mentors and mentees

Larry Ambrose

A PERRONE AMBROSE ASSOCIATES PUBLICATION

Common Sense Mentoring

PERRONE-AMBROSE ASSOCIATES, INC. PUBLISHER

Deerfield, Illinois

ISBN 978-0-9777540-3-8

Acknowledgments

Without the encouragement, support, collaboration and simple permission of so many, this book would not have been possible. My business partner, Jim Perrone with whom I've traveled this road since 1973, has steadfastly supported my efforts to record what we have learned together, and has been, I have sometimes thought, a bit too convinced of my talent. I will never forget that faith.

Noreen Gorman never ceases to amaze me by her ability to grasp the meaning of what I am trying to express and has been invaluable in helping me find the better word, the improved phrase. Simone Nathan's undying positivism has encouraged me to experiment with literary forms that at first seemed risky. Thanks to Marsha Montgomery, Senior Attorney and coordinator of BP Law Department's mentoring program, whose sharp-eyed reviews contributed crucial real-world guidance.

Writing this book has consumed nearly a year and a half. Present for all of the fretting, the rewriting, and the long hours closeted with my computer has been my wife, Karen. When I lost my momentum, I decided that I would go the library regularly to write and rewrite. She never tired of my preoccupation with the project; indeed, she could be relied on to prod, "Aren't you going to the library today?" And off I'd go to resume the chore. I don't know about other writers, but without that sustenance and her incisive editorial reviews I know I would never have completed this little book. Thank you, my love.

Foreword

Two things I've learned in over twenty years of working with mentors and mentees:

A great mentee never forgets a mentor.

A mentor never forgets a great mentee.

Great mentees help shape great mentors. I have met mentors of every stripe – executives, engineers, attorneys, nurses, nuns, organizers, teachers, chefs, foremen, you name it. Every one of them has been concerned about being a good mentor and has worried about living up to expectations. They have wondered, "Will I do this right?" "What'll my mentee expect?"

I have also known a great many mentees over the years – both novices and highly experienced specialists. They have worried, "Will I be a nuisance to my mentor?" "What can I ask of a mentor?"

I've told them all not to worry about it, that if they are blessed with motivated mentoring partners, all they need to do is make themselves available and show genuine interest. That fact has proven true in the overwhelming number of cases I have encountered.

Common Sense Mentoring is about those mentees and mentors with whom I have been privileged to work. I have learned what mentoring really feels like from them, even as my colleagues and I were teaching them about mentoring. This book is dedicated to them and to all of the mentors in my life.

This is not a how-to book. It is my attempt to give you the feel of mentoring, to address the little questions, those bugaboos and puzzlers that mentors and mentees experience, which are often more important than the grand mentoring principles.

I've known some great people and have had wonderful mentors in my life. My stories about them appear at various spots throughout the book as *Interludes*. Writing these sketches of my mentors has renewed my sense of their influence on me and their importance in shaping my growth. I include them in this book to suggest how you can learn from your own past mentors and to celebrate the significance of important people in your life.

Common Sense Mentoring is salted with stories, tidbits, admonitions, and advice – collected from real mentors and mentees. Particular offerings are labeled "For Mentors" or "For Mentees". Read them all. Knowing what I'm telling your counterpart can only help you and will be worth your time.

So read the book in any order you wish, but read it. If you're a mentor, read it with your mentee. If you're a mentee read with your mentor. Re-read it and see if you don't agree that:

- A mentee who has an agenda and the drive to pursue it cannot fail.
- A mentor who listens, invests time and keeps commitments cannot fail.
- A mentoring pair dedicated to each other and to their mutual success cannot fail.

Larry Ambrose

Contents

Prelude - Watching Charlie

When I think of my dad Charlie I think of work and silence. He was raised in the country and went through eighth grade three times, once because he hadn't before, and twice more after the crops were in and there was nothing for a 14 year-old to do on the farm in the winter. Going to the high school would mean six miles over mud roads and his old schoolhouse was only a mile.

After service in World War I, my dad did whatever he could to make a living: farming, threshing, gas station attendant, tire repair, handyman, carpenter - any job there was. He and my mother raised their three oldest children through the 1920's and 30's. I came along at the end of the Depression when my dad was 47 and nearly defeated by the worry and strain. I remember him saying that he was proudest of always having a job of some kind. He may not have been paid as promised, but he had always worked.

As a father he didn't say much as I grew up. Evenings, beneath our basement's insistent low ceiling my dad prowled his grotto of a workshop, honoring the invisible border with my mother's canned tomatoes, washer and clotheslines. Upstairs we could hear him as he talked out a plan for some project or other. He would take out his spent chew of tobacco and throw it in the old wash tub he had placed beneath his workbench. That tub remained there until he went to the VA Hospital for the last time decades later.

When he did speak he meant it and was sneakily funny. I was immensely amused by his impish sense of humor but I was also a little scared of him. My dad could freeze all of us kids in place with a glare that seemed to thinly mask a fury at life itself. I don't think I ever once crossed him because I was sure I wouldn't live to tell about it, but I should have known better. The one time he spanked me - at my mother's command - he sat right down and cried.

My father was not a philosopher or teacher, he was a doer and I absorbed how to move and how to just be by observing him. He possessed a fierce capacity for concentration and his focus and involvement with his work was my never-spoken lesson. With my two brothers and sister long out of the house, I worked alongside him as he shingled our house, built a new porch, and fashioned rock walls for our back lawn and gardens. It wasn't to teach me, it was because he wanted help and kids were for helping. He let me hang around him in his basement workshop, holding wood for him as he put it through the power saw. "Keep your fingers out of the saw, kid. Watch the blade. Push the wood all the way through before you reach for it," he'd say through his ever-present cigar.

Any self-designed little project I wanted, he helped me with: a wooden pistol, a soapbox racer, a golf bag carrier out of an old water pipe and two recycled wheels, even a very strange lounge chair for my college room. From my dad I learned you could take on a first-ever project that others said you were crazy to try, struggle with it and make it come out right. And I learned deep ethical values by listening to what upset him.

I remember one night he came home from his carpenter job, complaining how the bosses were cutting corners on a home build-out. To save money they would skimp on materials in a way that the homeowner would never detect. The foreman had told him to place the studs inside the walls 16 inches apart instead of the standard

14 inches, to use less wood. He'd say, "That goddamn house is going to fall down one of these days. I tell 'em but they pay no attention." When he added on to our house, he put the studs 12 inches apart. I revisited the house 50 years later and it was as good as new, not a wrinkle anywhere.

As reticent as he was, my dad would launch into stories about his and my mom's families and about his single guy times in the Army. His humor was so quick and spontaneous that I can't remember any of it. He never told jokes but his unique takes on situations and people always left you smiling and shaking your head. Any sense of humor I possess, I got from him. He was also profane and sometimes grouchy because the world and its ways often scared him.

My dad was never religious and deeply doubted the virtue of the pretentiously pious, "They go to church on Sunday so they can lie, cheat and steal the rest of the week." But he was a good man and true. Charlie never spoke lessons to me, but he lived out his values: Work hard. Do your best. Don't cheat anybody, ever. You become less of man by cutting corners. He taught me to lean into work, to give quiet care, to persevere at all times – no matter what, and to put sugar in my coffee and salt in my beer.

Charlie, my dear dad, showed me how to be a person. He will always be my life's role model.

For Mentors

The mentor's first lesson

A few years ago a new staff consultant, whom I'll call Jan, joined our firm. Shortly after she arrived, I offered to serve as her first-year mentor. She happily accepted, though she may not have felt she had much choice, as I am a senior partner. Nevertheless, she seemed genuinely excited about a mentorship with me, and we got together for our first meeting about a week before the traditional Christmas week off. Jan had organized her holiday week down to the minute. She and her fiancé would fly to Vermont for Christmas and a day of skiing with friends, then on to a spa for two days. After that they would be off to Boston for the history and the art museums, and home by January 2. I thought, "Do it while you're young, kid. A week on a beach would suit me fine."

Experience has taught me that many people put more creative energy into planning their vacations than their careers. Inquire about vacation plans and you might hear a description like Jan's, but ask about career and you may get little more than generalities. Granted, careers are more complex than vacations, but the analogy does hold some water. If it's not going to happen next week, it's hard to relate to it. People are hard-wired to navigate the foreseeable and to put off anticipating what's over the horizon. At the same time, every mentor wants a mentee who has her plan together and can articulate what she needs and wants. But don't be disappointed if your mentee can't do that right out of the gate.

Indeed, Jan had not thought very much about specific goals for her career. I remember thinking at the time that she could have a great future as a vacation planner. So, instead of what I thought would amount to one sit-down to clarify her mentoring plans, we spent four fruminous sessions grappling with the basic issues: what Jan wanted from me as her mentor, what skill and abilities she wanted to develop or polish, and what she needed to master in her first year at the firm.

But in the process we both learned a very valuable lesson. I had wanted to get started on the so-called real mentoring – helping her to make progress on her plans, but we couldn't do that just yet. We both had to learn that if Jan didn't have a plan, the act of getting one was the real mentoring she needed at that time. It took four sessions, but once we got things defined, we were able to launch our mentoring year and make real progress.

Lesson One: Your first mentoring responsibility is to start where the mentee is, and if she's nowhere, start there.

A beam from the sky

When I'm training new mentors I like to ask if that morning they had received a beam from the sky imbuing them with new wisdom and knowledge, now that they are mentors. Of course, they all smile and say no, that such a thing is ridiculous. Most mentors worry if they'll be good enough. They hope they'll have the right answers when their mentees ask for help. The typical new mentor wonders if he must now display some special insight or acuity not expected before. Likewise, a first-time mentee may have the same unrealistic idea - that his all-knowing mentor will give him the answers.

All you know is what you know, and that's fine. Don't worry about it. Somebody wanted you as a mentor, so you must have something that someone needs. Once your mentee lets you know what he needs and you start dipping into your knowledge and experience, you'll find that you know a lot more than you think you know; in fact, you'll be amazed. Relax, it'll come. Be comforted by the fact that your experience will also tell you when you should refer your mentee to someone else who may have an answer, approach or suggestion that you don't. That's mentoring, too; it's called "referral mentoring."

It's hard to screw this up

If you think mentoring is mysterious and difficult, it will be. Mentoring is a lot of things, all aimed at giving the mentee what she needs. There are no hard and fast rules, except to always stay in full-attention listening mode. Sometimes you teach; sometimes you coach and sometimes neither, just talk, or spend time together, maybe on a task. About the only way to screw up at mentoring is: 1. Don't Meet Often, and when you do, 2. Don't Listen, and also, 3. Don't Keep Your Promises. That'll do it. Any additional thing you may do, even the clumsiest effort that keeps your mentee's best interests squarely in focus will spell success.

I recently read about a technically gifted violinist who was told by his professor to give up on a concert career because he "had no interest or inclination to make someone else's thoughts or emotions his own." He could not get past his concern for himself. He could not develop empathy for the audience. Thus he could not communicate to them because they felt no vital connection with him. Your mentee must feel your affinity for her and her concerns. When that connection is completed, the mentoring becomes natural and can't fail.

What I get by being a mentor

I'm convinced that mentors should benefit as much as mentees do. If you don't get anything out of the whole adventure, your mentoring motor will run out of gas. Of course, it helps if you get a kick out of helping someone accelerate her progress. If you don't enjoy that aspect, my advice is to get out of mentoring as soon as humanly possible.

So how do I benefit by being a mentor? I am filled with appreciation that another person believes that I represent value to them.

Mentoring reawakens my senses. I re-teach myself the important lessons I've learned as I prepare to answer questions, to make suggestions, to teach someone else.

My only mission is to help my mentee become more able, so I concentrate more clearly on how to accomplish that – through listening, clarifying, probing and challenging. Focusing on these coaching skills carries over into all of my relationships. I believe it makes me a better person and more interesting to be around.

Mentoring forces me to re-open my mind to a wider range of alternatives and ways of thinking. I become more creative and more thoughtful, and that rubs off on all my habits, judgments and decision-making.

Mentees who have grown up in different circumstances than I help me look at things I might ignore or never face. I've had mentees who are younger, a different race, gender or culture, and who hail from worlds that seem exotic to me. These mentees have gifted me with a spectrum of views, values, norms and ways of thinking that I never would have celebrated.

My mentees have been blessed in ways that I have not, and they have mentored me.

So, if you're interested in dividends like these, become a mentor.

A couple of questions

What would you like your mentee to be saying about you a year from now?

What can you do to make that happen?

For Mentees

The mentee's first lesson

One day, out of the blue, I received a call from a young man who had seen our web site. He asked me if it is okay to ask someone to be his mentor. The mentor he had in mind was a vice president in a different department. The caller struck me as a very ambitious young man and I asked if he thought the person might be receptive. He said he didn't know, so I suggested that he contact others who know the executive better than he. I did add that in my view, most people who are asked to be mentors would be honored to do so.

He asked, "Would I just ask him right out?" I said yes, but was struck by this assertive young man's sudden hesitancy at the thought. I requested that he call me later and let me know how it went. He never called.

On reflection, if I had it to do over again I wouldn't make the same suggestion. I had no business advising him as I had. It is very daunting to just ask someone to be your mentor – not impossible, just daunting. I now tell people to do what one of my colleagues did. One day, after we had known each other for about a year, she said to me, "You've been a great mentor to me. You always listen and get right back to me when I ask for ideas. It's been just great. I always feel I can ask you anything." I was surprised and happy to learn that she thought of me as a mentor. I said, "Thanks. I'm a little surprised, but I'm really glad to help."

That very day I started to feel like a mentor to her, and I began to think of her as my mentee. She made me her mentor, and we're still in regular contact.

Lesson One: Make someone your mentor by asking for advice, ideas, and coaching. After awhile, find a way to tell him what a great mentor he's already been to you. Guess what? You'll have a new mentor.

What you'll get

People are always asking me if they should have a mentor. I tell them, "I can't answer that, but I can tell you what you'll miss if you don't have a mentor."

- You won't have the benefit of hearing a different point of view.
- You'll miss the opportunity to think out loud and test your ideas with a partner.
- You will not have your own devil's advocate to keep your thinking straight.
- You won't receive suggestions from an experienced person devoted to your enrichment.
- You won't be challenged in new and different ways.

Why do you want a mentor?

People want mentors for myriad reasons:

- Learning the shortcuts - how things really get done.

- Networking.
- Getting no-strings-attached advice.
- Learning more about themselves.
- Dealing with issues they might resist looking at.
- Having a partner or friend to talk to in confidence.
- Getting the best out of time and effort invested.
- Getting hints on how a mentor might approach things.
- Learning more about the ins and outs of career development.

What could a mentor do for you?

Don't give up if you're turned down

Persistence, and a little courage, may be necessary to get the mentor you want. I have an acquaintance, I'll call him Tom. Twenty-five years ago Tom was smart enough to see what a mentor could do for him. Back then we didn't call them mentors. Maybe we didn't call them anything – perhaps 'adviser' or 'sponsor' or 'a guy'. Tom wanted 'a guy' for career advice. The guy he wanted happened to be a certain high ranking, gruff, senior partner in his law firm. He worried that he might get turned down, but thought it couldn't hurt to ask. The partner was about 20 years older than he, smoked cigars in his office and didn't suffer fools gladly. Tom got an appointment and went in, where the guy sat, cigar in his mouth, staring at him. Tom told him he would like to work alongside him in order to "learn from him." The guy took the cigar from his mouth and said, "No," like a flyswatter.

"Oh God," Tom thought; "Now I've done it." And he turned and left quickly. He confessed later he thought he must have been crazy to ask in the first place but he couldn't stop constructing the picture of the benefits he could get with this man's help. So even though it was now very apparent how risky it might be, he went back again about a month later. "No," swatted again, and this time it sounded even louder than the first time. "Why did I do that? I must be nuts," he worried. But Tom kept thinking about it and didn't want to give up. Another tasteful waiting period and one more time, but this time the gruff answer was, "Okay".

Then the guy demanded, "You got any goals? Do you want to be something? You want to be a partner? An expert? A singer? A deep-sea diver? What?"

"Well. . . ," Tom hesitated.

"Come back with some."

Tom did, and that partner, now retired is still his mentor today, all these years later. Tom realized that the guy wanted to be sure he had the guts to keep at it, because that's the kind of mentee he wanted.

What are you made of? How bad do you want it? Bad enough to take a risk like Tom did? Bad enough to work at it?

You're at the helm

Probably the most common mistake mentees make is failing to define a core idea that drives where they want to go and what they want to be. You're the captain. Take your stance at the wheel. If you learn nothing else, learn that you can decide what you want, you can do what you have to do, and you can bend your reality to your will.

A mentor can't do it for you. Every successful person has made demands and has made known what he needs. He has sought help unselfconsciously and has experimented, making errors without shame. Every successful person has self-generated the energy and hard work necessary to stay focused and persevere. Thomas Edison said, "I have never made a mistake. I have only learned."

Ask yourself:

- What opportunities do I want a mentoring experience to give me?
- Where do I want to be at the completion of my mentoring voyage?
- What will be different for me then?
- Do I really want that?
- Will I be ready for it?
- What does my gut say?

Interlude - The Light of Gads Hill

I hadn't anticipated the surprise that greeted me as I entered Gads Hill Center for my introductory interview that late August morning. The place looked like a lower west-side warehouse, but I walked in and it gleamed. The waxed floors and the banisters glistened and an atmosphere of quiet determination announced that this was a place of purpose. Could this be an ordinary inner-city settlement house?

I came to this community center to work part time for room and board as a graduate social work student, fresh from rural downstate, as green as grass. If I had wondered whether I was really in the city, the hurtling trains of the Chicago elevated just ten feet outside my window sat me up in bed and trumpeted the fact all night long.

"Wait right here, the woman in the glassed-in office said when I introduced myself. "Miss Schwiebert will see you in a few minutes."

And when Miss Schwiebert did appear, I looked up and swallowed hard. Snow-white hair haloed an iconic face, proclaiming style but not fashion. She was tall and indefinably intimidating, and you could tell that she knew it. Years before, Meta Schwiebert left small town Iowa for Chicago as a young social worker. In time, Miss Schwiebert - no one would dream of calling her anything

*but that – came to define everyone's image of the com-
plete professional, the guiding spirit of the finest settlement house I have ever seen. She carried herself as the
role model that she was conscious of being and she
breathed the fire of mission into the place. She simply
would not allow failure.*

*My interview with her that morning was quick and per-
functory, leaving me convinced that my hiring was due far
less to my sterling qualities than to her having made a
commitment to the university's placement center. But
she didn't find enough wrong with me to turn me down,
so I began my "professional career," teaching kids wood-
working and counseling groups of tough Polish neighborhood boys. Eventually I got used to the El trains and to
the neighborhood kids and my reeducation proceeded
rapidly.*

*One of my groups was the Junior Wildcats, street-wise 18
year-olds who had to put up with me in order to use the
settlement. It was the era of pipe smoking and grownups
smoked pipes, so to be men the Junior Wildcats smoked
pipes and pretty much ignored me. At one of our first
meetings, held in an upstairs room filled with donated
chairs and tables, Jimmy Vlcek and Casey Lewandowski
were showing off their pipes and Jimmy asked to look at
Casey's. Of course, to appreciate a guy's pipe you had to
take it apart and Jimmy broke Casey's pipe. Now what? A
fight? Or, an "Uhh, that's OK?" I had no clue, and I was
supposed to be the "counselor".*

*Where I came from, everyone knew you and what you
were doing or ever had done, and you made amends by
saying you were sorry and offering to pay for repairs.
Casey looked startled. The others locked their gaze on
Jimmy. Without missing a beat, Jimmy took out his pipe
and said, "Here, break mine." Then Casey said, just as
quickly, "Nah, forget about it."*

Right then and there, I knew something different was going on here, some street rule for getting along, completely foreign to me but I knew I'd better pay attention. Jimmy's offer was enough. His willingness to sacrifice his pipe evened the score for the moment and it was back to business as usual. The best thing for me to do at that moment was to keep my mouth shut and go with it until I got my feet on the ground.

Would I ever gain the seasoning to be confident in this new world with its strange codes of ethics? Would I ever have the élan and self-assurance of Miss Schwiebert who could effortlessly sooth the old and the young with her mere presence and stanch a gang fight with her redoubtable glare? She barely had to speak.

But she did speak to us in our work, and she led us with high expectations spiced with a dash of compassion. But she was tough and could be severe, but never cruel, and I always felt cared about. Soon Miss Schwiebert introduced me to the fabled, fearsome weekly program conference, one-on-one with her. Summary notes on each counseling session were required and reported personally to her. Terrifying at first, these inquisitions transmuted into my favorite time of the week – report, defend, learn, reconcile, stretch and perhaps get some rare praise.

Miss Schwiebert fully expected well-considered answers and would always ask the question that took me a step deeper than my superficial preparation: "What were your reasons for doing what you did?" and "What will you do next? What will that accomplish?" She gave clear answers to my questions and expanded discussions with exactly the challenging teaching points a novice needed. And all that time I was thinking to myself, "She came from a small town just like I did. She made it. I'll bet I can too."

Miss Schwiebert created a world of culture and challenge inside that settlement house. She held monthly dinners *for the staff in her small, elegantly warm apartment with its dark reds, browns and rich wood, her very private quarters. Miss Schwiebert reigned at each dinner with grace and deliberation, simply assuming that everyone there would contribute something compelling to the conversation, which ranged from current events, to patrons of the settlement, to professional ethics. Many years later, I remember these scary and stimulating dinners through the lens of a country boy whose experience had never included anything of the sort.*

My step through the Gads Hill door that August was a passage through the armoire to the other side, where awaited a new world of discovery in which people can achieve the unpredicted, live out higher expectations, and reside in an informed universe. Miss Schwiebert gave me the best of gifts. She placed within my grasp the hope and the possibility of surpassing myself.

Just a Little Bit

Mentors tell me they worry because they think they're supposed to work miracles. "What if I don't measure up? What if I don't prepare my mentee to do great things?"

I've done a lot of mentoring, and I've never dramatically transformed anyone. I'm not that powerful. I try to make a little bit happen every time I talk with a mentee. I try to make my mentee a little stronger, a little bit more independent. A little bit more able to create his own options, make his own decisions, and solve his own problems. I'm no genius, but I can push a little bit in the right direction, ask a helpful question, or leave the person feeling, and thinking a little smarter. And you can, too.

Listening with your satellite dish

I know instinctively if I like a person. I also know immediately whether he's listening to me. I may not know why he's listening, I'm just glad that he is. One theory goes that it takes less than four seconds for a person to make up his mind about someone, so people decide pretty quickly about people who don't listen.

Many humans listen poorly, but it doesn't have much to do with any famously touted 'listening skills'. It's more about bad habit and inattention.

People send signals by every means - words, body language, facial expressions, super subtle body and facial messages. These bits of information are coming a mile-a-minute, and guess what, you are picking them up, maybe unconsciously - through your ears, eyes, and even your gut, your "whole body satellite dish". But if your attention wanes, is interrupted or divided, your satellite dish gets disconnected. You know what happens to your TV picture when your dish is malfunctioning. It won't be long before you're on the phone for repairs.

Keep your satellite dish plugged in. Guard against outside distractions and resist especially your internal "distraction factory". The average person lazily tolerates internal interference, thinking about something else, preparing her response, judging the other person - general brain chatter. Instead, concentrate on getting interested in the other person. Pay full attention; listen to him, not yourself; hear with all your senses. Make sure your satellite dish is hooked up.

Sherlock Holmes, the great detective, was asked how he was able to see what others almost always missed. He replied, "I have trained myself to notice what I see." You, in turn, can train yourself to notice what you hear.

Try this: Following a first conversation with someone, ask yourself how you would complete this sentence, "Based on what I've heard you say, this is what I think is important to you: _____." Then say it aloud before a mirror. How does it sound? Could you say it to that person? If you were to say it to him, how confident are you that you'd be pretty close to getting it right?

Sunday afternoon

Think about your mentee on Sunday afternoon. This is my way of saying that your mentee should be on your mind often, not only when he pops up before you. I think that's a real challenge for us mentors. Now and then I realize that I haven't thought creatively about my mentee for some time. That's forgivable and pretty inevitable in a busy world. But you should try to include your mentee in your thoughts enough to allow time to deliberate on what you can offer the next time you talk. Think about a question you can call and ask him, or an idea or suggestion you could make. Don't always wait until your next meeting, or until he asks for advice.

When I'm mentoring

When I'm mentoring, I get so into it that I don't think about my own troubles. It's a nice break.

I'm a mentor! Now's my chance!

One of the best things that can happen to you is someone asking you to be his mentor. Every time I'm asked, my mind floods with pride, optimism and wonder that someone thinks I could help. Anyone who's been asked for aid, even if it's for a little short-term coaching, knows the feeling – a person wants to spend time learning from you. But watch out. Don't get impressed with yourself. More than one mentor has thought, "Someone recognizes that I know my stuff. I'm a mentor! Now's my chance to wow him."

Don't go there. This is exactly not the moment to display how much you know. The only thing you should try to demonstrate is how well you can tune in to your mentee's wavelength and how accurately you comprehend what he needs. Perhaps what he requires is your vast store of beneficial wisdom, and maybe not. It could be that all he lacks is a sounding board for his own great ideas. Maybe what he needs is to develop his own wisdom. His, not yours.

You're no substitute manager

If you're mentoring a person who works for someone else, it's obvious that your mentee already has a manager. He doesn't need another one. You might not agree with what his manager is doing, how she is leading, her decisions or positions on issues. You're not a substitute boss, and it's not your job to second-guess or criticize his manager in any way. You know only what your mentee tells you. Your only calling is to serve as an additional resource for him. That's all. In no way should you complicate his relationship with his manager. You don't have first-hand knowledge. You don't know the whole story, so you have no business agreeing or disagreeing with what his manager is doing.

What goes on here stays here

Every mentee needs to be able to trust her mentor. She must be confident that what she says to you will go no further. This means that you must not betray to anyone what you and your mentee are discussing. And if she works for someone else, you will not reveal the content of your conversations to her manager, even if he asks you. Being a mentor means being true and trustworthy. As they say in Las Vegas, "what goes on here stays here."

A good mentor . . .

Will never quit on you if you don't quit on yourself.

Will give you what you need, maybe not what you want.

Will challenge you and support you at the same time.

Your mentor needs you

You can be a great mentee even if you don't have a great mentor. The same isn't true for your mentor. She can't even be a mediocre mentor without you. You're the one who gives the whole thing its energy. If you have something you want to get - a goal, a skill, or a little savvy - you can find a way that your mentor can help. But if you don't have desire and an agenda, your mentor is stymied. She has nowhere to go, nothing she can do. In a way, you have to be the hero of your partnership. You can even be your mentor's hero.

Once I had a mentee who didn't really want a mentor, but his company required it. I tried and tried, I called him, I emailed him, I tried to set up meetings, I asked him what I could provide. At first, he humored me a little and we met a couple of times, but no more. I was disappointed in myself. It must be me, I thought.

But I got over that. I called and left one last message for him. He didn't call back and that was that.

A great mentee can make a mediocre mentor into a good mentor. But a mentor, no matter how great, cannot make a poor mentee into anything but a former mentee.

57-43

I got into a dispute once about who's responsible for making a mentoring partnership work.

One argument went like this – "The mentor is the leader. After all, she is the one who has the knowledge and knows what the mentee should be doing."

Another took this position – "The mentee is 100% responsible. After all, it's his career, and he should make sure he's getting what he needs. He's got to be the driver."

I like a third argument – "Both mentee and mentor are accountable. They have 57%-43% responsibility." You must understand that you are majority stockholder in the partnership, at 57%. Still, the mentor, with 43% of the stock, holds a strong equity position. You must contribute mightily to attaining your goals and the mentor must stand ready to provide whatever help she can to support and assist. As in any partnership, if performance begins to sag, all partners are on the hook to take action.

Am I a nuisance?

Get in contact with your mentor regularly and often. Don't worry about being a pest. She'll let you know if you are. Then you can clear the air.

A question

Do you really want frank conversations, out-of-the-box thinking, and new challenges to your ideas? If your answer is yes, to paraphrase Bette Davis in the movie All About Eve, "Fasten your seat belt, honey. It's going to be quite a ride."

Network

Become active in a professional organization. Ask your mentor for ideas and suggestions for getting out there and networking.

Interlude - An Extraordinary Man

Noontime, November 22, 1963. Sgt. Herbert Thomas is tapping me on the shoulder in the mess hall. "Sir, would you come outside for a moment?"

Outside, he tells me, "President Kennedy has been shot and wounded."

"Killed?"

"Nobody knows yet."

The sky falls on my head. My god, I'm a U.S. Army officer and the President is wounded and could actually die! My insides scream, "Get over to Battalion HQ!" On the way, I say a little prayer of thanks that Colonel McGarity is in charge. There may indeed be no atheists in foxholes.

The Army was short of officers and it wasn't fair. New Infantry lieutenants were supposed to spend two years of seasoning, perhaps in charge of a 44-soldier platoon – "the men" in the all-male combat Army. Three months into my service at age 23, I was handed a full Company of 250 bewildered, perpetually exhausted basic trainees, many separated from me by no more than a year. "I'm not ready," I thought. But the same thing had happened to thousands of other wet-behind-the-ears officers. I had done nothing to give the impression that I was suited for such responsibility and, of course, neither had any of those others who shared my dilemma. Fair was not the issue, the Army needed officers and that was that.

Earlier that same year, in May, I had already survived eight months as a Company Commander when I was told we were getting a new Battalion Commander. A West Pointer of all things. I thought, "Oh swell, a by-the-book, career-climber. This can't be good."

Academy officers I had known carried themselves with a taut air of privilege. But Lieutenant Colonel Paul McGarity was cut from different cloth, much of it un-starched. No spit and polish and a bit paunchy with a posture that begged straightening, he ignited memories of a favorite professor. So, naturally I imagined he had been put out to pasture in this out-of-the-way basic training job and I expected to smell the odor of a decaying career. Not true. Possessed of a dusty-boot self-assurance, and blessed with relaxed common sense, Col. M. proudly held an ironic view of the Army. He practiced his belief that the Army is only people and an officer's job is to care for them as sacred human beings, not as property or as weapons. He revolutionized our young-officer comprehension of service and protected us so we could live it out as he practiced it.

Company Commanders personally sign for all unit property, including buildings, equipment, weapons and ammunition. I bore sole accountability for my trainees, and four rickety World War II fire-trap barracks, an orderly room with worn-through floors, a garage of a supply room and a greasy mess hall, along with 250 old rifles and ammo. The buildings were propped on cinder blocks at each corner and were spread over an acre of sandy former ocean bottom, their peeling paint turning upward like a schoolgirl's yellow curls. If anything caught

36

fire or disappeared, they said, I'd have to be promoted to the rank of General to pay it off in my lifetime. Naively, I swallowed it whole and was stomach-cramp petrified for all of the eight months until Col. M. came on the scene.

When I finally dared ask about the life sentence I might face, the Colonel just chuckled low and said, "Don't worry too much about that, these shacks have long since exceeded their life expectancy." Then he added, "The men and the weapons - take those utterly seriously. Pay attention to them and you're all right. And always make sure the men eat first. You need them more than they need you. We can always get another Second Lieutenant."

But Col. M. made sure he didn't have to get another lieutenant. He knew he had a group of very new, barely mature Company Commanders and that he had to grow us and grow us fast and the best way was to give us responsibility and tap open our minds and our courage to act on our own. I could go to him for help at any time. I could bring up a problem and he would always start with a challenge question: "What do you want me to do?" He would give me a look that told me I had to decide what I really wanted from him or if I really needed what I thought I needed. He made me choose and in the choosing I had to get in touch with how much responsibility I was taking on my own. A natural listener, he not only listened, he could read me and could tell when I was "not-saying" something I wanted to say, and he would dig it out of me. Col. M. wanted it all. He wanted my arguments, too and if I held back he pulled them out of me, so it got to the point where we would get into some real debates, and I kept growing.

And growing up became very important on November 22. Clearly as shocked as any of us at the news from Dallas that Friday and knowing no more than we did, Col. M.

kept all four of us Company Commanders with him in his office and taught us it was best to wait for instructions. When at last the feared announcement of the President's death came he settled us all down - there would be no special alerts, but normal activities would be on hold. The assassination was a numbing tragedy that threatened to overwhelm us, but we got busy working on how to inform our troops and control against panic.

An ordinary senior commander would have taken over and not allowed a bunch of young lieutenants to handle such an explosive moment, but not this man. We jointly discussed alternatives, and though frightened, we argued that we should each inform our own Companies and he agreed. The President was dead. But we, and he, knew that managing our own companies was our command responsibility and he allowed it. We went over what to say and how it should go.

Almost paralyzed I returned to my Company, had the more than 200 men called together and stood in front of them to present the terrible message, my voice catching more than once and finally escaping into "Now a moment of silence." It was one of the most horrifying and signifi-cant moments in my life, one allowed me by Col. McGarity. As I dismissed the troops, I looked around for the Colonel and he wasn't there. He stayed away and didn't watch over me. He trusted.

My active duty tour drew to a close the following June. I never enjoyed the military, but I could feel myself becoming a man, growing in confidence because this man simply expected me to do my job and cleared obstacles from my path. I was ready to get out and get on to the next thing, but Col. McGarity had other ideas. Without my knowledge, he had nominated me for General's Aide de Camp, a prestigious post, for which very few are recommended. It bowled me over, but I would have to extend for at least a year if I accepted it, a very dis-

*agreeable prospect. The offer deserved serious considera-
tion, though, and my wife and I thought long and hard
about it. But I knew inside that I didn't belong in the
Army and couldn't take the job. So I declined.*

*I have never regretted the decision, but always hated
disappointing Colonel McGarity. Thinking back about it
through the mist of the years, I realize it was he who had
given me the self-assurance to turn the offer down, and I
thank him for that. When I gave him my decision, he told
me I was crazy to forego the experience. "Surely we
didn't do all this work just to have you end up a civilian,
did we? Well, if you're going to be one, be a good one."*

"OK, Sir, I'll try," I said.

Who calls whom?

Perhaps your mentoring get together was canceled at the last minute and you haven't scheduled a new time to talk. Or maybe your mentee asked a question and you haven't been able to get back to her. Could be you've been wondering about your mentee's commitment to the relationship over the past month or two.

What now? I've had many moments like these and have been confused. She hasn't called. I haven't called. Should I feel guilty? Doesn't my mentee like me anymore? Am I not doing this right? Should I be angry? Disappointed? Besides, isn't the mentee supposed to take the lion's share of responsibility? It's her career after all.

The easiest thing to do is nothing. You probably have many, many other responsibilities without including chasing a mentee. Don't be fooled. This may be an early sign that the honeymoon period is coming to a close. This is the point at which your partnership has some questions to answer. Is it going to continue past the novelty stage? Can it become a relationship that survives and thrives even when you're both too busy and the bloom is off the rose? The question is who calls whom? Is the ball in your court or her court?

Answer: It doesn't matter. If you're not hearing from your mentee, don't wait. Call her and set a time to talk – and talk only about what's going on in your partnership, not about the current mentoring topic. This is the time to check out how the partnership is doing and what you need to do to get through whatever doubts or misapprehensions that one or both of you is having. Now's the time.

Hold a mirror to your mentee

Perhaps the greatest gift you can give your mentee is to share your frank impressions with her. This means to tell her how you see her, what you know to be true about her and offer it, no strings attached, without requiring her to agree. Your impressions of her began to take shape from the very first moment of your mentoring partnership. You are there solely for her benefit. So you can be the mirror that reflects your true picture of her, to help her form as accurate a self-image as possible.

It is a priceless gift for a mentee to receive her mentor's description of how she comes across, what her effect is on others, how she may be unintentionally getting in her own way, or what she does most effectively. Any mentee whose mentor has held up the mirror for her will attest to how unusual – and how incredibly helpful it is to get the straight scoop on herself. I always say, "If your mentor won't tell you, who will?"

No commiserating

If you're a mentor, you should never be guilty of commiserating with a mentee.

Barb just wants advice, so you give it. Sally doesn't want responsibility for a screw-up, so you agree it's not her fault.

When you're the mentor, everything is different. No commiserating allowed. Let's say you're Barb's mentor. Does she need the advice, or does she want a shortcut? And what's your motivation? Do you want to keep it light, to feel good, to do for Barb? Or is your motive to get Barb to do for herself? Your job is to give her what she needs, not only what she likes.

You're the teacher insisting that a student dig, analyze and reach conclusions. You're the tough baseball manager demanding that your batters run out every pop fly. You're the drama coach observing the fine points of performance with laser honesty.

Advice also has its place. The teacher instructs the student how to do analysis. The manager shows the player how to bunt, slide, and avoid the pick-off play. The drama coach demonstrates a technique. And they all expect to see results. So go ahead and give Barb advice if she needs it to succeed, but not because she wants it, just to feel comfortable.

Anything that builds your mentee's strength or power, you should do. Anything that increases your mentee's dependence on you, you should avoid.

Getting feedback

I always ask mentors if they want their mentees to give them feedback on how they're doing the mentoring job. They always say yes. Then I ask them if they think they'll get the feedback, and they always say no.

I ask why, and they say that a mentee probably would feel it's inappropriate to "complain". Mentees have lots of feedback they don't give their mentors: the mentor talks too much and doesn't listen well, she's not available enough, she thinks her job is to solve all the mentee's problems, etc., etc.

Mentees have a tendency to do something called "assigning authority" to their mentors. They put them on a pedestal. Most mentees make the assumption that their mentor is a mentor because of rank, or expertise, or knowledge, or experience, or wisdom, or some other grand virtue. Nobody wants to correct someone who sits on a pedestal.

So, how do you get good information on how you're doing? Three easy things you can do: Solicit, Solicit and Keep Soliciting. The first time you meet with your mentee, get an agreement that he will give you feedback on how you're doing as a mentor. Tell him that you're going to Solicit that feedback often. Second, Solicit feedback as a common practice in your regular conversations, but don't expect a lot very soon. He'll need frequent signals that you're serious about this. Third, Keep Soliciting and eventually your mentee will give you more and more honest reactions, and the more you listen, the more you'll get.

You can make it easier for him if you ask for specifics. Examples like, "Tell me one thing I can do more of - or begin doing that would help you most," or "How about something I should do less of - or stop doing?" or "I wonder if I got locked into giving too much advice the other day. How was that for you?"

People can deal with questions like that.

Stop! Hold that advice

Human beings are hard-wired to give advice. Show us a problem and we want to solve it. We tend to think that that's what people want from a mentor. Even after all my years of coaching and mentoring, I still start to formulate my ready recommendations as soon as someone brings up an issue or problem. Mentors, you need to stop right there. Hold your suggestions and learn how to coach, to draw ideas out of your mentee and ease the way for her to solve her own problems, perhaps with some indirect assistance from you. Hold your avalanche of advice. Ask a question instead. Use your mentee's momentum, not yours, to get to her finish line, not yours.

When the honeymoon's over

It's their fourth month of mentoring and they go upstairs at a favorite coffee shop, back to a windowless corner to avoid distractions. They haven't spoken in more than a month, and each pretends that the mentoring is going well.

Sheila asks how Jack is doing. Jack replies, "Fine, things are going pretty well." And they go on and the meeting is OK, not bad. Cordial. The listening is good, some review, some suggestions, but not much insight, it turns out. Jack wonders, "What is Sheila thinking? Is this her idea of what mentoring is? Maybe I was wrong to expect a lot. Getting together is nice and all, but back when we started it sure felt like it was going to be more than this."

It's a common story. Two busy people with good intentions and many obligations get into a mentoring partnership, but then lose concentration along the way and begin to drift. You don't feel much connectedness and seem to be only playing the roles of mentor and mentee. As the mentee, you wonder if your mentor has changed her mind about you and that she wishes she weren't in the relationship. You haven't met for a while, so now you're not sure what to do. You're at a loss as to what to say about all of this, and you think maybe it's just as well to leave it alone.

Honeymoons. They all end, but should the partnership fall apart as a result? It's time to take action.

Here are some suggestions for snatching victory from the jaws of defeat.

- If you haven't spoken with each other in awhile and you feel the momentum draining, call your mentor.
- Before ending any conversation, talk to each other honestly about what your discussion has accomplished or hasn't.
- In addition to regular meetings, agree that you'll meet once every three months just to talk about where the partnership is and where it's going.
- Compare impressions about how you're doing with each other and what each is gaining from the partnership.
- Broach the uncomfortable subject. Say: "I'm wondering about (how often we're meeting),(the quality of our sessions),(how we are communicating) and I don't know if you're feeling the same." That'll get something started on a positive note, without falling into the blame game.

Surpass your comfort limits

Chicago Bears founder, George Halas said, "Nobody who has given his very best has ever regretted it." People who make a total effort, especially when it's scary, have a "surpass-your-limits" orientation. They concentrate on being great, not just good enough.

By becoming a mentee, you've decided to think in new ways, try new things, and explore untested avenues. You've resolved to challenge yourself, to live outside your comfort zone, and decide not to settle for being average. You will try to think and act "bigger," to test your courage and your commitment to excel. Willingness to surpass your comfort limits means that you'll ask your mentor to challenge your view of what is possible, push you to do just a bit better, and insist that you stretch toward your next horizon.

You can reprogram yourself to live to your full potential regardless of the start you got. People do it all the time.

Take on something new

Attempt to write a proposal for a new trend or technique to present to a group or a decision maker. Use this proposal as a challenge to do the best writing you've ever done. Your mentor will give you the support you need.

You can help your mentor

"Would you like to hear an observation?" my mentee Chris asked me during a conversation.

"What about?" I said.

"About you."

"OK, shoot." ('Hmmm. Something's up. I wonder what he's got to say.')

"Well, it would help a lot if you could hold your opinion a little longer till I can get my idea out. There, I said it. Is that OK?" ('Please don't get mad.')

"I do that, huh Chris?" ('Do I really jump in? Maybe I do.')

"Yeah, you do," Chris said, his voice quavering a little.

"How is it a problem? Uh, I jump in so soon, like I think I know everything and you could benefit so much by listening to me. Is that it?"

"That's a little strong. I just think if you allow me more openings to think out loud, I might come up with something good, you know?"

"I hear you. My wife tells me that all the time." ('And now you, too, huh?')

"I was worried about saying this to you."

"You needn't have worried, but it's a strong habit and hard to break. I'll try to deal with it, and I need some help. Can you flag me when I do it?"

"You sure you want me to do that? Cause you do it a lot." ('OK now Chris, don't get too comfortable'.)

"Yeah, sure. If it'll help you and if it'll help me do a better job." ('I guess I really need to work on this.')

It's always scary to give feedback to somebody, especially to your mentor who is giving of himself. Who wants to be ungrateful to a mentor? But you could do what Chris did. He screwed up his courage and dared to say what needed to be said and what I needed to hear. Even though it was a little hard for Chris to say, I really appreciated it.

What made Chris's feedback to me so helpful? First, he asked my permission to say something and got it.

If I had said no, he probably would have stopped right there. Then he clearly told me what I could do that would help. Great. And then he asked if it was OK to give me feedback like that, showing he was aware that he had done something that might cause some upset. After Chris did all that, we were off to the races with a good give-and-take about how we'd work on my behavior in the future.

How did it go after that? I was fine for a couple more conversations, then I fell back on my old habits. So Chris brought it up again, and I was good for a few more conversations.

And that's the way it goes, folks. Nobody changes a habit overnight and forever. Try as we might, we fall back, and need to be reminded about the same thing over and over again. So don't be afraid and don't get upset about needing to give the same feedback repeatedly. Just stay in the fray. We're all imperfect humans, even mentors.

Look in the mirror

Ask your mentor for feedback. Especially ask about your impact on others. Believe it, your mentor will have useful observations for you on this.

What scares you most?

My idea of myself changes a little whenever I get an unexpected insight or learn something new about who I am. Putting your self-image to the test is

49

daunting and can be scary, but that's what mentees do. To grow is to flex your self image. None of us is very objective when it comes to sizing-up ourselves, and your idea of yourself may not be all that accurate anyway. So why not take a new look?

Sailors talk about sailing "close to the wind", heading as directly into the wind as your boat and its sails will tolerate without capsizing – pushing the limits of your boat and yourself. Sailing close to the wind will test you big time. Risking takes courage. Learning takes practice. But it gets easier, less scary, and then so natural that you wouldn't want to live without the buzz that comes from testing yourself. Flex your idea of who you are, and you'll become a constant learner.

Get creative

Challenge yourself to come up with a creative solution to an ongoing problem. Use your mentor to help you think outside the box.

Interlude – Eddie and Fran

Half-glasses at half-staff, he read half-interested, grimaced, stopped half-way through and tossed it on the desk. "What do you expect me to do with this? It's crap." The "it" was free-lance writer Fran Atkinson's investigative article on corruption and payoffs in state contracts. Fran had to get it through Eddie O'Donovan, the law school-trained associate editor of the muckraking 2d Look Magazine. "Why do you waste my time and your time? This is going nowhere. Do it over or drop it."

Eddie had no time for amateurs, which is what he thought of Fran. Slight, dark-haired, sad-eyed and hard-working, Fran would be the first to admit she was new at political writing, but she was zealous and committed to bringing the lawless to heel. Whether Eddie respected her didn't matter; she, Fran Atkinson was investigating injustice and simply had to go through him to get into the magazine. And he was happy to stand in her way.

She hated going to the 2d Look offices for reviews with Eddie. She'd wait in the bullpen. He'd come out in his own sweet time, late as if she had nothing better to do than await an audience with him. "Well, we gonna fight again?" he'd grin. He was a tree-stump of a man, thick and straight up and down, no waistline, no neck and tough-guy Irish to the bone. He loved to mess with the unschooled, who called him Fat Eddie behind his back.

"Come on. In the back," he'd say every time. And he'd aim himself ahead, crouched like a lineman, his pink face framed by a thatch of orange hair. Lunging, pigeon-toed in headlong trudge, he would lean into his destination. Eddie would charge at everything, every problem, and at any unprepared solicitor, with or without rank. But he was a hell of a writer and a damn good judge of what would fly.

"What's wrong with it?" Fran asked nervously, feeling overmatched by his attitude and bulk, which he used effectively.

"Don't ask me that. You're supposed to be an investigative reporter, or at least that's what you call yourself."

"Now you're just being insulting," Fran fought back.

Eddie stopped, "There's no proof here. Why should I believe what you're telling me about these guys? Fix it."

As she walked out of the building into the friendly sunlight, a stark contrast to the depressing, paper-piled, dented file cabinet 2d Look digs, she wondered why she volunteered for this abuse, why she ever thought she could write. Eddie O'Donovan among the clutter and dust of that place – she wondered what makes him so great, where does he get off talking to her like that? Because he can, that's why.

When she got home and back at the laptop, her last grilling from Eddie repeated itself: "Why should I believe what you're telling me about these guys?" Rereading her article, Fran saw the weight of the evidence pointing clearly to guilt; it was enough for her, she knew the state supervisors were guilty of taking bribes, she knew it. So she set out to rewrite it, digging deeper into her notes, finding some more incriminating details she had not thought necessary.

Another appointment with Eddie, another wait in the bullpen, another trudge to the back office. This time Eddie actually shouted, "Now you're insulting me!" he yelled. "You take the same unsubstantiated garbage, process it through another disposal and think I'll accept it? More! Give me more, give me something new that might just make me think you actually got off your duff and checked your facts!"

"But it's obvious these guys are dirty. Any child could tell that," Fran countered.

Eddie looked at her over his glasses, "Then go tell their mothers. But tell me the facts. Now get outta here." And he threw the draft at her.

"I'd like to kill him," she muttered, heading for a decaf mocha, skim, no whipped cream and a Danish with her fiancé Sam, a college teacher.

"So Eddie's an animal," Sam said. "The world's full of them. But could he, by some cosmic quirk of fate, be right? Could you do more?" She knew one thing for sure, Fat Eddie would not stop her.

* * * * * * * *

As she drove slowly into the ready-mix plant's parking lot in the city's Lower River district, Fran could see the ripples in the dirty water that flowed slowly past and wondered how many bodies had been dumped there over the years. It was a perfect place, isolated and lined by tall weeds, sunken far below road level, tough to see anything going on there if you're just driving by. She looked across the river at the Wolf Point Yacht Yard and thought of the skippers sailing by, oblivious to what ghosts might lay in the river's depths. Putting the *thought away, Fran went looking for Joey Caro. She had interviewed him before but had some new questions for him now.*

Fran third-degreed Joey, then later faxed Eddie her revision to bypass the agony of witnessing his growing disappointment as he read. When they finally met, Eddie offered, "So you did a little investigating this time. Lovely. Now go get what you need to make the case and prevent us from getting sued. Come back when you have something." He twiddled his fingers at her, "Bye-bye." Sweet progress, maybe.

Back to Joey, who after a little more persuasion pointed Fran to Paulie Ronko and Manny Cruz. They were a great help, connecting the dots to two agencies and three other shady firms. Finally she had her story - something to write, and she wrote it nonstop all night. Fran couldn't wait to call Eddie O'Donovan. She got the appointment, and went in.

"Come on. In the back," Eddie said as always, but promptly this time. Fran would never get over the cluttered pathway through the cubicles, the dirty carpet, the obstacle course of cartons and boxes. "You've been working for a change," Eddie said when they sat down. "You got two sources for all this?"

"Yes. Paulie and Manny confirm Joey's story and I talked to three others who all check out, plus I had two state representatives run away from me at full gallop."

She looked up in surprised relief as Eddie said "Alright, good, let's get into this." She and Eddie spent the next two hours examining all the incriminating details, each coming up with new approaches to the article. "Now, you need a rewrite. It looks like you must have written the thing in a fever in about half an hour. You're a good writer, you just weren't as good as you could be this time. Do it over like we talked and fax it back to me. If it's OK, it'll go in the magazine next month."

Eddie never really changed, but Fran did. She had found a way to keep up with him and even occasionally a half-step ahead, which was what she suspected he had wanted from the start. They collaborated on 11 more articles over the years, fewer of late because of Eddie's severe diabetes, which finally forced him to retire.

Eddie died early on March 18, and his wife called and went over to see Fran that same day. She told Fran that he had dictated a note to her just before he passed away. Fran's eyes filled and she smiled as she read it:

"Fran, there'll be a funeral and I want you to write my obituary. You're the only one who can do it right. Now get on it and get your facts right. You've only got 24 hours before deadline. Eddie."

Postscript

Fran made deadline. Eddie's obituary appeared on March 20. She added this author's note at the end:

"The day Eddie died a number of us lifted a farewell pint to him at a local bar. We talked about his toughness, his stubborn will and our fear of him. But there was also the spirit of the man, the well-disguised sweetness you would discover if you stuck it out with him. Most of all though, we remembered what he had taught us, insisting that we do better than what we thought our best could be. Eddie was my mentor. But he would have turned red and screamed at me if I had ever called him that to his face. So, Eddie, here it comes, you were the best mentor I ever could have had, and I'm going to miss you."

Off the hook

You're just the mentor. If you're not your mentee's boss, you're off the hook. You're only there to help. You have no direct responsibility for your mentee's performance. Although you surely want him to do well, your only agenda is his growth and learning. You are free to concentrate on lending a hand – teaching, advising, listening, probing and coaching – with the sole objective of helping your mentee become as competent, self-confident and strong as possible. And, because you're not his boss, he has the freedom to use your help or ignore it.

We all talk about favorite aunts, uncles, grandparents (if they don't spoil us), neighbors, clergy and teachers bestowing tough love and encouragement. These mentors leave unforgettable legacies, the pictures of life, and they're free to do and say what they do precisely because they're "off the hook".

Continuous partial attention

I ask people to tell me about their best mentors. The president of a worldwide pharmaceutical supply company gave the best answer ever. He said, "When I was with my mentor, he made me feel like I was the only person in the world to him at that moment. Whenever we talked he was always right there, never in a hurry or distracted."

Lives are full of distractions. Multitasking has replaced simple effectiveness as the watchword of the day. People have become very good at paying incomplete attention to lots of things at once, instead of deep attention to one thing at a time. Microsoft executive, Linda Stone, names this habit "continuous partial attention". Wired into the web, cell phones and Blackberries, our very capability to stay connected 24-7 makes us feel bad or lazy if we choose to disconnect, even for a short while. How many times have you received a call on your cell in the middle of a conversation? Research shows that it will probably take several minutes after an interruption to regain full attention to the issue you were discussing.

What if that intrusion came during a mentoring session? In mentoring, the one-thing-at-a-time rule is crucial. Mentors who tune in completely at these moments are like the Amazon forest nature guide who is totally in sync with the sounds, smells and visual pageant surrounding him. He never misses a plant, an insect or animal and points out each, highlighting its relationship to all the other beings in the forest. He is in communion with all that he senses. As a mentor, you are a kind of nature guide, and the mentee's world is your sole environment for the time you're together. Can you resist the magnetic pull of continuous partial attention? Will your mentee say that he feels as if he is the only other person in the world when he's with you?

Don't be surprised

In my opinion, people have little or no use for inveterate advice-givers, those self-appointed teachers who always have an agenda for you. They want you to see the world as they see it. It's fun to notice how surprised those folks are when you're not so interested in the lessons they love to share. "Nobody takes advice anymore," they lament, "not like the old days." Truth is – nobody has ever happily taken advice, except when it has hit directly at a need that they have strongly felt. People want to grow and improve, and will welcome information that supports them in that. But don't be surprised if you offer your dearly held advice and meet with a polite, half-hearted response.

You can't teach grown-ups what you think they ought to do or know - not unless they agree first. Ask yourself how you have learned new things. Did you happily absorb first-time lessons just because they were conferred by some erudite, perceptive sage? If someone did lay a recommendation on you and it stuck, why did it stick? I doubt if that advice would have endured if you had not already identified it as a need or an interest, regardless of its origin.

If you place an Amazon.com order, you gladly welcome the delivery-person. The same goes for learning. You have to feel that you've ordered it. Adult persons need a prior interest in something if they are to welcome the lesson, otherwise nothing happens – nothing real.

So don't be surprised. Work hard to learn what your mentee wants and needs. Probe, dig, push back – get absolutely clear on his requirements and the reasons for them. Once you get in touch with what is important to him, the mentoring gets easier, more natural, and the advice more valued. Then your mentee will place his order and happily open the door when you deliver. Just don't be surprised.

Show your 'self'

My father used to say, "Everybody's dumb about somethin'." But mentees often think the opposite about their mentors. Deep inside, your mentee may have a tendency to think you were hatched as the finished product, destined for success right from your auspicious start, and unfairly endowed with knowledge, grace and style that she was not. Ask any mentee if that's true and she'll deny it. But answer it honestly for yourself and you'll admit, as I do, that your mentors looked pretty extraordinary to you. It will be no different for your mentee.

Like everyone she'll suffer self-doubt and worry. She'll wonder if she's taken the right course on a problem, but she may imagine that no uncertainty has ever crossed your path. Perhaps worse, in some small way you might feel tempted to reinforce that impression. Nothing could be more inappropriate. You need to be a role model, yes, but not some unattainable ideal. Your mentee may think she wants perfection in a mentor but will hate it if she gets it. You should want her to say to herself, "My mentor is good and I think I could be at least that good or better if I keep working on it." A mentee who has no hope of catching or matching her mentor will eventually lose interest and give up.

Unless you're superhuman, you've had struggles, doubts, and setbacks. Let her see that. Level with her that there is a good bit you don't know and that you consider yourself a work in progress just as she does. Share your feelings about yourself, your career and your philosophies of life. Friends of singer Tony Bennett say that at 81 he's like a kid, eager to learn everything he can. They report that he doesn't feel or act like a superstar and excitedly soaks up everything he can from performers much younger than he. That's what keeps budding singers flocking to him for mentoring and inspiration.

The more your mentee experiences you as a fellow human being who is continuing to learn and grow, the more open, receptive and resilient she'll become. And wouldn't it be great if she turns out even better than you?

One thing can make a big difference

There's no way to predict what is likely to have a big impact on a mentee. You can't plan it in advance, the opportunity just presents itself, and you do what you do and say what you say.

One of our consultants and I were on a training trip to London and were taking a walk during a break in the day. We were strolling along chatting when she mentioned a guy she was currently seeing. She said this relationship felt different from any she had had previously, and that she was really crazy about the guy. Married for many years by then, I naturally wondered what she was going to do about it. But I said nothing, minding my own business.

Then she said that she was afraid to tell the fellow how she felt because "it might scare him away." Throwing caution and good taste to the wind, I just blurted out, "If you tell him you're crazy about him and it scares him away, he's going to run at some point anyway. All you can do is to love him and hope he loves you back." I thought, "Now I've done it.

Should've kept my mouth shut. I don't belong in the middle of this." She just stared at me for a moment with a look on her face and we left it right there.

Some months later, she called me to say she was getting married and it was all because of me. She had taken in what I said and told him about her feelings, and his were the same. So I got all the credit which, of course, I didn't deserve.

You're probably thinking that what I did was no big deal, that anyone would have done the same. Yes. And that's just the point. You or I could see possibilities in her situation that she could not. She needed another person's perspective, offered by someone who cared about her. The next May we attended her wedding, and I still regularly get overblown credit for her happy state in life.

My wife and I gave them a kite for their wedding, and they still call us whenever they fly it.

Go slow to go fast

Typically, people don't say what they mean and don't express what they feel. It seems that there's too much risk of revealing a weakness, a flaw, a fear. We're all pretty much the same that way.

I often ask groups of mentors, "If a mentee were to say to you, "They don't pay enough around here," what do you think she's really saying?" Every single group has immediately answered that she's not getting enough appreciation. Unless you're her most trusted confidante, your mentee is not likely to confess her sensitivity about too little appreciation. She's more likely to take the safer route of complaining about pay and hope you catch on, and be dissatisfied when you don't.

Don't take the bait. If you react to the first thing out of her mouth with an answer or suggestion, your response is 90% sure to be irrelevant and off the point. Recognize that simple fact. Listen, probe and seek out what her important issue truly is. As you listen and question more, you'll get closer and closer to understanding her and her issue, and you'll be in a much better position to give her the help she needs, instead of the help you wanted to give her in the first place.

We all want to help, and we're impatient to solve problems. We want to go fast. Spending time to get an understanding of the real issue feels slow, but if your reflexive reaction is off the point, going fast makes no sense. You'll have to come back and start over. A miner can't make real progress until he hits the seam of coal. So be a patient geologist and dig for the real issue. It's better to go slow to go fast.

Here's a go-slow drill you can do on your own. Tune in to a daytime soap opera, or if you can't stand that, a primetime drama. When one of the characters describes a problem or asks for help, don't think about the advice you would give. Instead, quickly write down five questions you could ask the person to get to his real issue. Even shout your questions at the TV screen, if you're alone. Form the habit of probing. You can do this.

Call your mentee

Call your mentee and ask him a question. It'll show him you're thinking about him. It'll stir the pot and fire you up.

Own up to your strength

As a mentee, it is essential that you take a serious inventory of your strengths. All people have strong suits, but most of us find it easier to notice things we need to improve on. Mentees need to inventory and own up to their talents, their muscle, and their vigor. You need to build your long-term success on a foundation of your capabilities and your energy.

Look at what you do instinctively well. Do you relate to people easily? Do you see complex issues with great clarity? Do you bring a ferocious work ethic to everything you do? Recognizing your own power is the GPS system that will steer you through blind allies and around dead ends. Once you find your direction, you can choose experiences that will both test you and allow you to develop yourself further. Knowing and celebrating your talent gives you the optimistic energy to pursue the right challenges.

When you respect your strengths, and self-assuredly share them with your mentor, you help him know you better and understand how best to help you.

Co-create

A cup of experience is worth a gallon of advice. I vividly remember my most important experiences and I replay and replay them, extracting new lessons each time: working out racial discrimination disputes in Chicago, depending on Army doctors to save my newborn son's life, running a business partnership built on trust. But advice? I recall only a little of the advice I've received – and only if it was something that immediately interested me, or an idea that worked perfectly right away. Advice, instruction, and suggestion are talk. Experience is action.

People learn best by doing. You can make that happen in your partnership. Every time you and your mentor talk, require yourselves to "co-create" - produce ideas or projects that can generate experience for you. Be sure that both of you contribute input. For every idea the mentor has, you should produce two. You will find that often you'll co-create at least one thing that you can try. It might be a challenging on-the-job project. The plan can be that you will seek permission to try an innovative solution to a problem. It may be an off-job activity, volunteering or adventuring. The habit of co-creating will focus your work together and surprise you with results that neither could have anticipated without input from the other.

Progress comes in little pieces

I've learned that permanent progress takes time. That "overnight sensation" you heard about last week most likely put in years of work and preparation. Have you ever tried to change a habit? Quit smoking? Lose weight and retain your new shape? The first five pounds are easy. What about the next twenty-five?

You pick up the bat and, after a few tries, you hit a curveball. That was easy. Try it again tomorrow, or next week. Not so easy now is it? Keep the weight off forever? Yeah, right.

I don't recall any single experience that has changed me permanently. Some incidents have introduced me to new directions or different thinking, and over time I've altered some behavior traceable to them. I think that's what really happens. I never believe someone claiming to be "transformed" by a single event or inspiration.

When I was in my twenties and in the process of changing the world in short order, I had a boss who used to say, much to my chagrin, "Larry, do you know what progress is?" I would roll my eyes, "Here we go again." He would place his finger on the edge of his desk and move it the slightest bit along. "It's going from here . . . to here. It's progress as long as you're going in the right direction." And I've learned he was right. When you understand this, you'll make real steps forward, and they'll be enduring ones.

Sessions with your mentor

You hear it all the time – have regular sessions with each other. But, in my opinion, you shouldn't meet only because you said you would. Both of you should know in advance why you're communicating that day. If you can't tell someone why you're having a meeting with your mentor, call it off.

When you do talk, have a plan. Mentoring sessions work much better with a little structure. I like to use a simple 3-step plan:

First Step: Review

- What's happened since last time?
- Successes and accomplishments?
- Challenges that remain?

Second Step: Review Learning

- What worked well?
- What will you do differently next time?
- What can you do on your own?
- How can your mentor help?

Third Step: Agree on Next Steps

- Co-create a next opportunity, activity or assignment.
- Set a time and date for your next conversation.

Start at Step #1 in your next session and repeat the process. Believe me, this little scheme will see you through.

Protect your sessions

Every mentoring pair I've met has told me the same thing. Protect your mentoring sessions. If you communicate consistently you may not have the perfect partnership, but if you don't talk you'll definitely have an unsuccessful one.

Mentoring is extra. It's helpful, it's wonderful, but it's extra. You're busy. Everybody's busy. Very few people think mentoring is a bad idea, but people don't always follow through on good intentions, and mentoring pairs still falter.

Take special care to maintain your partnership. You'll need to protect it because all of your other obligations conspire to derail your best intentions. Unprotected, it's very likely that your mentoring conversations will slide off the radar screen. So set a schedule to communicate, say, once or twice a month. Put the appointments on your calendar. To be sure, you'll have to cancel one once in awhile, but since you have them written down you'll tend to honor them, or at least reschedule if you have to cancel.

Call your mentor

Call your mentor and ask him a question. He'll love it. Mentors want to be useful.

Join a task force

Volunteer to serve on a project committee or a task force. Ask your mentor for coaching during the project and go over the results with her. She will love that you're using her as a coach.

Interlude - An Inspiring Lady

Jeanne Barry died recently. She was 87, my wife's good friend, and one of the youngest people I knew. Three of my favorite women, all decades apart in age - Jeanne, my wife, Karen and their friend Jan - fashioned their own annual Fall Architectural Tour (the FAT tour) around the Midwest marveling at the work of Louis Sullivan and Frank Lloyd Wright. To save money, they all roomed together in a succession of small town motels, calling me in the evenings to help them resolve some silly dispute like the meaning of the word "vector," laughing and giggling like teenagers. They had so much fun learning.

Everybody loved being around Jeanne. I cherished the few times I got to be with her. It was not because she had a long career as mother of four children, reporter for a large metropolitan newspaper, public affairs director for a prominent university, traveling to every continent, sailing most of the world's oceans in a small sailboat with her son, and becoming a poet and novelist in retirement. It was because she was just so curious and non-judging about everything and everybody, especially you at that moment. Everything was OK with Jeanne, except when a restaurant didn't serve her beloved martini before dinner. That brought out the Irish.

She was not a cockeyed optimist but she welcomed each day with acceptance and celebration, and she inspired us to see that we could too. Jeanne seldom made statements or gave advice. She asked questions, and with unalloyed curiosity about what you were thinking and feeling. She never asked leading questions; she seemed to have no agenda except to hear you and learn from you. I never had the feeling that Jeanne was looking for me to give her the answer she had in mind. She just wanted to hear my answer, and that was fine with her. I learned about myself by answering her.

I can't say I knew very much about Jeanne's own life, she considered that less important than finding out about my life, my thoughts and feelings. Was it the newspaper training? Maybe. But I think it was something deeper and more in the fiber of her, materializing from her innermost desire to know and esteem others and the world. Virginia Woolf, said it well when she wrote that people who ask questions always have more to say than those who claim to provide the answers.

Shortly after Karen and Jeanne first met, as docent trainees for the Chicago Architecture Foundation, Jeanne was struck and seriously injured, at age 72, by a city bus. Their friendship flowered during Karen's many visits to her bedside. The mishap didn't stop Jeanne. She served many years thereafter, a little shakier from her injuries, taking visitors and Chicagoans alike on tours around the city. As she aged, we saw that the effects of the accident began to overtake her. Finally, a few years ago she reluctantly gave up her duties as a tour guide and settled into raising butterflies in her high-rise apartment and firing off letters to the editor about all manner of injustice.

We all loved being with Jeanne, and now she's gone. I wonder sometimes who will ask the questions and who will raise the butterflies.

For Mentors

The secret checklist

Some years ago I listened as a mentee spoke at a mentoring conference. She said, "I have always appreciated my mentor's advice and suggestions, but I found that I am most interested in how he thinks. He doesn't tell me how he thinks, he shows me."

If you were to ask me how I think, I couldn't tell you. Reflecting on that mentee's remarks, I realize that I've built up certain patterns that work for me – my "secret checklists" that guide how I think through problems, make decisions, and handle conflicts. But where did I put them? They're pretty far inside, in my "automatic pilot" that I go to almost unconsciously, my muscle memory. If I could find them, maybe I could share them with my mentees, and that could be much more valuable than the bushels of advice I pile on them.

I have found my checklists right under my nose. My thought patterns are revealed in the kinds of questions I ask myself when I make a decision or solve a problem. And I can show my mentees my checklists in the same way – by asking questions, questions that make them think according to a pattern of logic and problem solving.

So I ask questions like: "What have you tried so far? What has worked best? What alternatives do you

have? What's a reasonable goal for you? What resources do you need? How can I help?"

You'll ask your own questions your way, and they will
reveal your secret checklists. I'm sure you'll discover,
as I did, that your mentees are pretty smart when you
give them the chance to think. We're all familiar with
the adage, "Give a person a fish and feed her for a
day. Teach her to fish and feed her for a lifetime."
Whoever coined that saying hundreds of years ago
knew what they were talking about.

Putting the ball in play

The most valuable hitters in baseball are the guys
who "put the ball in play." They're not the home run
hitters, they hit fair balls and make the guys on the
other side chase them. They make the other team
work. They make some outs, but over a full season,
they get their share of hits and drive other runners in.
These hitters make a difference. You always feel
hopeful when these guys come up to bat.

Your job is to make a difference with your mentee, to
put the ball in play and see what she does. Your job
is more akin to bunting and singles-hitting than to
belting the long ball. Home runs belong to the hitter
and no one else, but the well-placed bunt sets off a
drama of running, sliding and scoring by the players
being moved around the bases by the hitter. That's
your job: setting off a drama of thinking, creating and
deciding by your mentee.

You swing for the fences when you shower mentees
with suggestions, advice and how-I-would-do-its.
When you want to get your mentee running the

bases, you bunt or go for a single – you spray fair balls, known as "no-agenda" questions, and ask her to go after them. No-agenda questions should never represent your point of view. They should never be leading questions. You simply place a question on the table, for example, "What did you learn by doing that?" or "What would you do differently if you could do it over?" and let her dig up her answer to it. Did you notice that I said her answer, not your answer? That's the crucial point.

Trial lawyers are taught to never ask a question for which they don't already know the answer. I teach mentors to always ask questions for which they don't have the answers. Your aim is to help your mentee become a better critical thinker and independent performer, not to help her do things the way you do. The world probably doesn't need another you.

Bunting requires practice. No-agenda questions demand practice, so work on them until they begin to feel natural. Here are some to work on:

- "What conclusions can you draw from that experience?
- "What was your greatest challenge in attempting that?"
- "What scares you most about trying this?"
- "What do you want to achieve in this next project?"
- "What is the first step you'll try?"
- "When will you get started?"

Push for action

Every time you and your mentee speak, try to get her to take a step forward, if only a short distance. Never end a mentoring session without pushing for an action – an action your mentee is ready to take or to at least try. Ask her what she will do between now and the next time you meet or talk, a new approach she is ready to use, a plan she can commit to, a schedule she will pursue, an outcome to seek.

Don't ask if she is going to do such and such. That makes it too easy for her to give you superficial agreement and get you off her back. Instead, ask "What are you ready to do? What's you're first step?"

Your goal is to get some evidence of her thinking and resolve. Once you've listened to her design for action, you can react by agreeing, encouraging or by more questions if you feel she needs further coaching.

The greatest thing since sliced bread

A huge truck was wedged in an underpass, its top crunched at the 13.5-foot clearance sign. Firemen, police and the department of public works were toiling mightily to extract it, but nothing had worked. A crowd gathered, people shook their heads, "They're gonna have to take the thing apart to get it outta there," someone said. A small boy and his dad looked on from the crowd, "Daddy, why don't they let the air out of the tires?" Maybe it was the little boy's lower vantage point, but he definitely had a different perspective and one that a fireman overheard and used to solve the problem.

A corporation in a mid-western city had a problem. Its elevators were too slow. The penthouse executives complained constantly about the long wait. The engineers reprogrammed the elevators into every configuration imaginable, express and local, elimination of little used freight lifts, speeds of ascent, to no avail. In a last-ditch effort to remedy the problem, the company offered a twenty-five thousand-dollar award to anyone who could create a solution.

The proposals flowed in, but they were just more of the same until one day it came, offered by a most unlikely source – a high school art teacher and her class. The offer was actually a request to attempt a two-week experiment, and if it failed, the company would owe nothing. The installation was made and the complaints stopped immediately. No elevators were reprogrammed, no new ones installed, no speeds altered. Only one thing was done: the entire elevator bank on the executive floor was lined with mirrors. That's it. The executives immediately stopped complaining about elevator delays. Problem solved, prize awarded, new art supplies were purchased for the school.

The guy who invented the bread-slicing machine didn't invent bread, and he didn't invent slicing, but he had the creativity to apply new alternatives to already existing know-how: bread and slicing.

You need not feel pressure to bestow revolutionary ideas upon your mentee. You needn't conjure never-thought-of concepts and fully realized approaches to thorny problems. Your job is to encourage her to discover alternatives, inspire new combinations of thought and action, and rouse her imagination to perceive the commonplace, using a new set of eyes. When you instigate and nurture the creative process and help keep its heart beating, your mentee's inventive fire will be stoked, and you'll be doing your mentoring job. Who knows, maybe she'll invent the best thing since sliced bread.

A 'not-mentor'?

Ruben Santiago-Hudson is passionate about his mentor, the late renowned playwright August Wilson. Mr. Santiago-Hudson is an Off-Broadway director, writer and Tony Award-winning actor who has both acted in and directed plays by Mr. Wilson. Wilson, who died in 2006 would have described him as a 'rooster', not given to modesty or humility. Mr. Santiago-Hudson agrees. He hasn't time to pussy-foot around. He goes straight into every challenge.

Wilson's life and work invoke a devout veneration in him, who finds himself voicing incisive Wilsonian wisdom almost out-of-body. He has even saved a last voice message from Mr. Wilson on his phone and continues to speak of him in the present tense. Santiago-Hudson describes his ongoing 'communication' with Mr. Wilson this way, "...I'm saying 'Look at me, look at what I did. Are you happy? Did I make you proud? Was I what you thought I was going to be?'"

Maybe Mr. Wilson didn't mentor him in the classic sense, through meetings and counseling. Instead, it seems that Santiago-Hudson latched onto the essence of him. He worked with Mr. Wilson. He observed him. He struggled to measure up. He tasted his genius. He savored the sweet wine of his life and his drama. He allowed Wilson's life and luminous devotion to his art to ignite the flame of his own. The true role model. The true 'not-mentor.'

Can you bottle that essence? Without bottling it up? Can you learn to be a not-mentor? I talk about my mentors, but a number of them were not-mentors. They just had natural, unselfconscious great moments that they somehow showed me. And now, more and more, I think they occasionally knew they were imparting a lesson, probably not taking it all that seriously, laying it out there for what it was worth. It was up to me to infer its meaning for me. If I did, fine. If I didn't, there'd be another chance sometime. I guess I was a "not-mentee".

Had my not-mentors been consciously trying, could they have made sure I retained what they intended? No. Could they have ensured that I learned one thing rather than another? No. My sister and I grew up together in the same household, with the same parents and retained utterly different life lessons.

Could my not-mentors have intentionally sent messages without destroying their spontaneity? Yes, I think so. I think you can be intentionally spontaneous. You can do what many of your own not-mentors have done. Start by noticing somebody you think has promise as a not-mentee.

- Allow this not-mentee to see you in spontaneous moments.
- Let her see you in action, warts and all.
- Allow your 'self' to show, unrehearsed.
- Don't miss opportunities to notice how she works, what she delivers.
- Volunteer an observation or suggestion here and there.

- Offer praise when you see her doing something well.
- Take the risk to offer an unsolicited critique on something you feel she could do more of, less of or better or if something she does is hindering her success.
- Suggest a challenge she might take on.
- Let her know that you feel she could handle greater things.
- Offer help in co-creating what she might try - a learning opportunity, a difficult assignment, a commitment to take new risk.

When and if she does ask for help or advice, respond beyond her expectations.

Don't worry about good behavior or style, just be your cantankerous, imperfect, brilliant self.

Challenge

"Please describe the single most significant experience in your career success." This question appeared in a research questionnaire presented to over 150 top business leaders. To a person, each responded by describing something he had survived - a challenge, an experience, a sink-or-swim accountability - something that got his full attention, a true test. When you think about it, you would probably give the same answer to the question. You wouldn't choose an experience that was "no sweat".

The same is likely true of your mentee. Go ahead, ask her the question right now. I bet she'll describe a challenge she was not sure she could meet. So don't be confused about whether you should be a little tough on your mentee. You're in a great position to offer challenges and to push her to try things she might never attempt had you not come on the scene. You have the opportunity to be remembered as the one who provided the test that made the difference in her career.

For Mentees

Dare to show your worst

It's important to let your mentor to see your best and your worst. It is essential that she sees your strengths, but she'll have more to work with if you also let her see your struggles. Be frank about your needs and doubts, and let her see your less impressive traits. You will be helping her to give you the feedback you need in order to take your next steps.

You may have to impress your boss, and you may want to appear successful to your colleagues, that's understandable. But don't get caught up in trying to make an impression on your mentor. If there is anybody you should not have to pretend with, whom you can confess your doubts to – or just be a stumble-bum with – it's your mentor.

Learn deliberately

I like to see a mentee squeeze everything she can out of an opportunity. Pursue challenging new learning opportunities. Stretch your capacity. Try out new approaches to broaden your perspective. Look for the learning in your successes and mistakes – all of them. Find opportunities, projects, and activities that can move you along a path of intentional growth.

Get in the habit of asking yourself, "What did I learn from this?" and "How can I use these lessons?"

Make yourself into a hero mentee

People often speak of mentors in heroic terms: "My mentor's advice turned my life around." "My mentor was instrumental in helping me take the risks that got me where I am today."

All well and good, but it would be more accurate to speak of mentees as the real heroes. It requires heroic courage to risk experimenting with new ways of living and working, to try things you've never tried before. Here are some ways you can become a heroic mentee:

- Open yourself to all possibilities.
- Decide to endure the uncomfortable for the sake of new experiences and growth.
- Identify where you need to do some growing, and share that with your mentor.
- Take permanent possession of your career path.
- Use your mentor's experience and seasoning.
- Seek and embrace your mentor's feedback.
- Dare to let your mentor see your worst.
- Drive the agenda.
- Know what you want and commit to act on it.

Try something difficult

Volunteer to take on an 'undoable' project, a task at which the last person who tried it failed. Tap into your mentor's coaching to help you plan and implement your approach.

How many mentors?

Though I have referred to "your mentor" in this book, I'm concerned that using such a singular term may give the impression that you should have only one mentor, or only one at a time. Not true. Collect all the mentors you need. Highly successful people repeatedly talk about their many mentors.

You might have a "formal" mentor, either as part of a mentoring program or because you have agreed to formalize a mentoring relationship on your own. That's fine, but don't limit yourself.

- Use "not-mentors" as role models.
- Ask a certain person to mentor you on a particular issue - perhaps an aspect of your behavior, skill or style that you need to work on.
- Request another's help on a single task or project challenge, and when the project is over, the mentoring is over.
- Be aware that every mentor will conduct himself differently depending on what you're looking for – formal mentors are concerned about helping on a range of issues.
- Not-mentors probably don't know you're keying on them so they just go about their business.
- Task or project mentors will concentrate specifically on the matter you've identified. However, you should not behave differently with any of these mentors.
- Have a clear agenda of what you want and need when you approach each mentor.
- Bring openness to change and a willingness to develop new habits of thought and action.
- Finally, cultivate your determination to get what you need and have high expectations that you can help your mentors help you.

Collect many mentors. The more people whom you view as potential teachers, coaches and resources, the faster your network will expand and the more possibilities you will discover.

Final Words

For Mentors

Find a mentor for yourself

You're not finished growing yet. When your mentee sees that you are still learning, she will find it inspiring.

For Mentees

Volunteer as a mentor

Mentor a kid. Find out how it feels on the mentor's side of the table.

About the Author

Larry Ambrose has been a mentoring and coaching consultant for more than 30 years. He, his business partner Jim Perrone and their staff at Perrone-Ambrose Associates have assisted hundreds of client organizations in making mentoring a key human development strategy. Larry has written A Mentor's Companion and The Mentoring Field Guide. He has also co-authored The Mentee's Navigator with Mr. Perrone.

Mr. Ambrose and his wife Karen live in Chicago.

Mentoring Products by Perrone-Ambrose Associates

A Mentor's Companion by Larry Ambrose, a managing partner of Perrone-Ambrose Associates, offers a journey through the mentoring interaction. It is a combination of behavioral menus and live dialogues between "high tech VP Ruth Merlin" and her mentee, "Manager Art Regent."

The Mentoring Field Guide collects the action checklists from A Mentor's Companion and puts them in an easy-to-find-and-use format. It will simplify the preparation for mentoring meetings with mentees and will improve Mentoring skills by making the use of best practices more consistent.

The Mentee's Navigator is a spiral bound handbook for people who want to learn and grow and take charge of their own careers. Learn the principles of Mentee Success; build a partnership with your mentor; track progress and chronicle your lessons learned.

The Mentors 2100 Audit is a 360° feedback tool which measures critical skills in the six key areas of supporting, challenging, pathfinding, empowering, double-loop learning and managed learning. It lets the individual know how he/she actually behaves as a mentor and coach. Each Audit packet includes: 1 self assessment audit, 1 supervisor Audit, 10 direct report/other audits, easy to use instructions, and a Results and Analysis Manual presented in a comprehensive, easy-to-read format.

The Mentor Self-Assessment allows mentors to reflect upon their mentoring behavior and skill and to develop a plan for self-improvement. The Self-Assessment evaluates the same critical skill areas as the Mentors 2100 Audit in a do-it-yourself format. The assessment can be used as part of mentor skills training or as a stand-alone tool.

The Mentee Self-Assessment is a self-scoring evaluation intended to assist in the knowledge and development of the individual on six competencies critical to a successful mentoring relationship. Employees will learn how they can be better mentees by examining their ratings on Receptivity, Self-Management, Self-Awareness, Growth Orientation, Resilience and Double-Loop Learning Focus.

The Compass for Mentoring & Coaching is a 6" x 8" card that provides mentors with a directional approach in conducting the mentoring session. The reverse side lists 32 questions and statements to assist the mentor.

The Mentors 2100 Series Pocket Prompter is a triple fold pocket-sized card for use when mentoring takes place away from one's desk. It lists competencies, questions, hints and reminders.

The Mentor's Bookmark is a 3" x 8" laminate which states in "commandment" format the practices of a highly effective mentor.

The Mentee's Bookmark is a 3" x 8" laminate which describes the 5 principles of mentee awareness that foster a successful mentoring experience. On the reverse side is pictured a lighthouse above "The Mentee's Navigator" with a Subtitle: Making Mentoring Happen.